Quantum Wealth Unlocking Financial -

Potential with Quantum Technology

By Ben Davis

Content:

Chapter 1: Understanding Quantum Technology

Exploring the basics of quantum technology and how it can revolutionize the financial world.

In today's rapidly advancing technological landscape, quantum technology stands out as a frontier that promises to transform various industries, including finance. Quantum technology harnesses the principles of quantum mechanics, which is the science of understanding and manipulating the smallest particles of matter and energy. Its potential is immense, and its implications for the financial world are both exciting and revolutionary.

To grasp the power and possibilities of quantum technology, it is essential to comprehend its fundamental principles. At its core, quantum technology leverages the unique properties of quantum mechanics, such as superposition and entanglement. Superposition refers to the ability of a quantum system to exist in multiple states simultaneously, allowing for exponentially more information storage and processing capabilities than classical computers.

With superposition, quantum computers can execute complex calculations incomprehensible to classical computers. Financial institutions can harness this power to optimize investment portfolios, model intricate risk analyses, and simulate market scenarios with unparalleled accuracy. Imagine the potential for generating substantial returns in a fraction of the time it would take with traditional computing techniques!

Quantum entanglement, on the other hand, is an elusive phenomenon that connects particles in a way that their states become intrinsically linked, regardless of the distance between them. This strange property has fascinating implications for financial security and encryption. By using quantum encryption, which relies on entangled particles, communication channels can become virtually impenetrable to cyber attacks. This revolutionizes the way sensitive financial data is protected, ensuring its confidentiality and integrity to a degree unattainable with classical encryption methods.

Furthermore, the field of quantum machine learning has the potential to revolutionize investment strategies. By leveraging quantum computers' ability to process vast amounts of data and identify intricate patterns, financial institutions can develop sophisticated algorithms capable of making highly accurate predictions. This opens up new opportunities for algorithmic trading, asset management, and financial planning, ultimately leading to enhanced returns for investors.

Quantum technology offers a significant paradigm shift for the financial world, but realizing its full potential requires overcoming various challenges. One such challenge is the preservation of quantum coherence, which refers to the delicate state in which quantum systems must operate to maintain their computational advantages. Any interference or interaction with the external environment can cause interference and lead to errors. Scientists are tirelessly working on developing error-correction mechanisms and finding ways to extend the lifespan of quantum coherence to enable practical quantum technologies.

In conclusion—oops! Sorry, there won't be any conclusions or summaries here. Just know that we've merely scratched the surface of understanding quantum technology's impact on the financial world. In the second half of this chapter, we will dive deeper into real-world applications and explore the potential risks and ethical considerations associated with using quantum technology in the realm of finance. Until then, stay curious and get ready to be amazed by the wonders that lie ahead!With the foundation of quantum technology set, let us now delve into its real-world applications and explore the potential risks and ethical considerations associated with its use in the realm of finance.

One of the most promising applications of quantum technology in finance is quantum-inspired optimization. By harnessing the power of quantum computing to process massive amounts of data, financial institutions can optimize complex investment portfolios more efficiently. Traditional portfolio optimization techniques often struggle with the curse of dimensionality, where the number of possible asset combinations exponentially increases with the number of assets considered. Quantum computing can mitigate this challenge by exploring a large number of possible portfolios simultaneously and identifying highly optimized solutions efficiently. This technology enables investors to find optimal allocation strategies that maximize returns while reducing risk.

Furthermore, quantum machine learning presents exciting possibilities in developing advanced predictive models for financial markets. By leveraging the computational power of quantum computers, financial institutions can analyze vast amounts of historical data, identify intricate patterns, and make highly accurate predictions about market trends. These predictions can enable algorithmic trading strategies that react to market shifts in real-time, enhancing overall investment performance. Additionally, quantum machine learning can assist in analyzing market risks and forecasting potential financial crises, allowing institutions to proactively mitigate potential losses.

However, as with any revolutionary technology, it is crucial to consider the potential risks and ethical considerations associated with quantum technology in finance. One primary concern is the security of quantum communication networks. While quantum encryption offers unparalleled protection against cyber attacks, traditional internet infrastructure remains vulnerable. As quantum computers become more prevalent, adversaries may attempt to intercept quantum signals during their conversion to traditional signals, compromising the integrity of the communication. Thus, the development of quantum communication infrastructure and protocols is vital to ensure secure financial transactions and protect sensitive data.

Another point of consideration is the potential impact of quantum technology on employment in the financial sector. The automation and advanced capabilities offered by quantum computing and machine learning algorithms could lead to job displacement in certain areas. However, it is worth noting that new job opportunities may also emerge as companies develop and implement these technologies. The successful integration of quantum technology into existing financial systems will require a comprehensive plan to handle workforce transitions and ensure the development of skills aligned with this new era of finance.

Ethical concerns also arise regarding the use of quantum technology in investment decision-making. As algorithms become more complex and capable of analyzing vast amounts of data, there is a need for transparency and accountability. Financial institutions must strike a balance between leveraging the power of quantum technology to enhance investor returns and ensuring fair and ethical practices. Regulatory frameworks need to evolve to address potential biases and unintended consequences that may arise from using advanced algorithms to make investment decisions.

In conclusion, quantum technology holds immense potential to revolutionize the financial world. Its applications, such as quantum-inspired optimization and machine learning, offer opportunities for enhanced investment strategies, risk analysis, and financial planning. However, it is essential to consider the potential risks, security concerns, and ethical implications associated with its use. The integration of quantum technology into finance requires careful consideration, collaboration among stakeholders, and the development of robust frameworks to maximize its benefits while ensuring responsible and fair practices. As we embark on this journey into the realm of quantum technology, we must embrace curiosity, open dialogue, and ethical decision-making to unlock its full potential and shape a future where financial potential knows no bounds.

Chapter 2: The Science Behind Quantum Wealth

Unraveling the quantum principles that underpin the concept of quantum wealth and its potential for financial transformation.

In the realm of quantum physics, where particles can exist in multiple states simultaneously and teleportation is no longer a realm of science fiction, there lies a profound connection between the quantum world and the concept of wealth. At first glance, these two subjects may seem unrelated, but delving deeper into the intricacies of quantum mechanics, we begin to uncover a remarkable harmony between the fundamental principles governing this mysterious realm and the workings of our financial systems.

Quantum wealth, a term that may sound enigmatic, encompasses the notion that our thoughts and beliefs have a direct influence on our financial reality. To comprehend this concept, we must grasp the quantum principle of superposition. In the quantum realm, particles can exist in a myriad of states simultaneously until observed. Similarly, our thoughts, emotions, and beliefs can exist in a multiplicity of states, each with its unique vibrational frequency. These frequencies, in turn, interact with the vibrational field of the universe, shaping our financial circumstances.

Entanglement, another fundamental principle of quantum physics, also contributes to the understanding of quantum wealth. It suggests that particles can become interconnected, sharing information instantaneously across vast distances. In the context of finance, this concept implies that our financial intentions and aspirations can become entangled with the infinite possibilities present in the quantum field. By aligning our thoughts and intentions with the frequency of abundance, we establish a profound connection with the quantum realm, expanding our reality and manifesting wealth in ways previously unimaginable.

Moreover, the fascinating phenomenon of quantum entanglement highlights the interconnectedness of wealth and consciousness. The renowned observer effect in quantum mechanics asserts that the act of observing a particle can alter its behavior. Likewise, through our conscious awareness and observation, we have the ability to influence the outcome of our financial endeavors. By directing our attention and focus towards prosperity, we fundamentally shift the quantum probabilities in our favor, opening doors to new opportunities and pathways to abundance.

Quantum wealth is not merely a theoretical construct; it has compelling scientific evidence supporting its efficacy. Researchers have conducted experiments using quantum technologies to enhance financial success.

For instance, quantum computers, with their extraordinary processing power, are employed to analyze vast amounts of financial data, identifying intricate patterns and trends that elude traditional computational methods. This enables investors to make more informed decisions, maximizing profits and minimizing risks, ultimately leading to enhanced financial well-being.

In conclusion, the underlying principles of quantum mechanics provide us with a unique perspective on wealth and its potential transformation. By understanding and harnessing the quantum nature of our thoughts, intentions, and consciousness, we can unlock the mysterious realm of quantum wealth. Through the principles of superposition and entanglement, we discover that our financial reality is intricately intertwined with the quantum fabric of the universe. As we continue our exploration into the depths of quantum wealth, we will uncover the practical applications and strategies that allow us to tap into this extraordinary power and unlock our fullest financial potential.

But for now, we have only just scratched the surface of this intriguing connection. The journey into the depths of quantum wealth is far from over. In the upcoming second half of this chapter, we will delve deeper into the practical implications and explore the strategies to harness the power of quantum technology for financial transformation. Prepare to embark on a voyage that will challenge your preconceived notions and open doors to a world of infinite possibilities. Stay tuned.

As we delve deeper into the realm of quantum wealth, we uncover practical applications and strategies that allow us to tap into the extraordinary power of quantum technology for financial transformation. Through the utilization of quantum technologies, such as quantum computers, we can enhance our financial success and unlock our fullest potential.

Quantum computers, with their exceptional processing power, have revolutionized the way we analyze financial data. By leveraging the principles of quantum mechanics, these computers can process vast amounts of information simultaneously, identifying intricate patterns and trends that were once elusive to traditional computational methods. As a result, investors are empowered to make more informed decisions, maximizing profits and minimizing risks.

Furthermore, quantum technologies enable us to explore new frontiers in financial modeling and forecasting. By harnessing the power of quantum algorithms, advanced simulations and predictive models can be developed, providing invaluable insights into market fluctuations and investment opportunities. With the ability to quickly adapt to changing market conditions, quantum-powered financial models offer a distinct advantage over their classical counterparts.

But quantum wealth extends beyond the realm of computational advancements; it also encompasses the transformative potential of quantum cryptography. Traditional encryption methods rely on complex mathematical algorithms, which can be vulnerable to hacking and security breaches. In contrast, quantum cryptography employs the principles of quantum entanglement to establish secure communication channels that are resistant to eavesdropping and tampering. By leveraging the unique properties of entangled particles, such as their instantaneous information-sharing capabilities, we can ensure the privacy and integrity of financial transactions, fostering trust and confidence in digital economies.

Moreover, the concept of quantum wealth can also be applied to the realm of financial planning and goal-setting. By aligning our thoughts and intentions with the frequency of abundance, we can manifest wealth and attract opportunities that align with our financial aspirations. Quantum visualization techniques, rooted in the principles of superposition and entanglement, can aid in programming our subconscious minds with positive financial beliefs and expectations. By immersing ourselves in the quantum field of possibilities, we tap into the inherent power to shape our financial reality.

To fully harness the potential of quantum wealth, it is crucial to embrace a mindset of openness and adaptability. The dynamic nature of quantum mechanics reminds us that the possibilities for financial transformation are not fixed or limited. Instead, they are ever-expanding and evolving, requiring us to continuously explore new frontiers and adapt our strategies accordingly.

In conclusion, the science behind quantum wealth illuminates the profound connection between quantum principles and our financial systems. By harnessing the power of quantum technologies, such as quantum computers and cryptography, we can unlock new avenues of financial success and security. Furthermore, by aligning our thoughts and intentions with the frequency of abundance, we can leverage the principles of superposition and entanglement to manifest wealth in ways previously unimaginable. As we continue to explore the depths of quantum wealth, let us embrace the infinite possibilities and embark on a journey of financial transformation.

Chapter 3: Quantum Computing and Its Role in Financial Systems

As we delve into the world of quantum computing, it becomes evident that its impact on financial systems is profound and far-reaching. Quantum computing, with its ability to process vast amounts of information and perform complex calculations simultaneously, has opened up a realm of possibilities that were once considered beyond reach in the field of finance.

Traditional computing systems, built on classical principles, have their limitations when it comes to handling complex financial data. These systems rely on binary digits, or bits, which can represent either a 0 or a 1. The power of quantum computing lies in its use of quantum bits, or qubits, which can exist in multiple states simultaneously due to the phenomenon of superposition, exponentially increasing the computational power.

This exponential increase in computing power has the potential to revolutionize financial systems in various ways. First and foremost, quantum computing enables more accurate risk assessment and prediction models. Financial institutions heavily rely on risk analysis to make informed decisions and mitigate potential losses. With the ability of quantum computers to efficiently process vast amounts of data, complex algorithms can be developed to assess risks in real-time, taking into account numerous variables and interdependencies. This would provide financial institutions with a deeper understanding of market trends, helping them to make more informed investment decisions and optimize their portfolios.

Furthermore, quantum computing could redefine digital security in financial transactions. Currently, encryption algorithms protect sensitive financial information. While these algorithms are effective against classical computing attacks, they could be easily broken using a powerful quantum computer. However, the same power that poses a threat to conventional encryption methods also offers a solution. Quantum cryptography, which relies on principles of quantum mechanics to ensure secure communication, can protect financial transactions from prying eyes. With quantum key distribution, where encryption keys are generated using random quantum states, financial systems can achieve unrivaled security that is virtually impossible to breach.

The potential of quantum computing extends beyond risk analysis and security. It could also optimize portfolio management by generating efficient portfolios that maximize returns while minimizing risks. Quantum algorithms can process an array of financial data and optimize asset allocation based on predefined criteria, leading to improved investment strategies and higher returns for investors.

Looking ahead, the emergence of quantum computing brings a host of exciting opportunities and challenges for the financial industry. By harnessing the power of quantum technology, financial systems can adapt and evolve, potentially revolutionizing the way we manage wealth and make financial decisions.

In the next part of this chapter, we will explore real-world applications of quantum computing in financial systems, discussing use cases and the potential impact as this technology continues to advance. Stay tuned for the next section, where we will dive deeper into the fascinating world of quantum wealth and its implications for the future of finance.Quantum computing has the potential to transform financial systems in numerous ways. In the first half of this chapter, we explored the revolutionary possibilities that quantum computing offers, from enhanced risk assessment and prediction models to redefining digital security in financial transactions. Now, let us dive deeper into real-world applications of quantum computing in financial systems and its potential impact as this technology continues to advance.

One area where quantum computing could make a significant difference is in the optimization of trading strategies. Traditional portfolio optimization relies on mathematical models that aim to maximize returns while minimizing risks. However, these models often face limitations due to the complexity of financial markets and the sheer volume of data to process. Quantum algorithms, on the other hand, can efficiently handle large amounts of data and solve complex optimization problems, leading to more effective and profitable trading strategies.

Another exciting application lies in the field of fraud detection and prevention. Financial institutions are constantly challenged by sophisticated fraudulent activities that can lead to significant financial losses. By leveraging the computational power of quantum computing, these institutions can develop advanced fraud detection algorithms capable of quickly analyzing vast amounts of transactional data and identifying potential fraudulent patterns or anomalies. This would enable early intervention and proactive measures to mitigate risks, safeguarding the integrity of financial systems.

Furthermore, quantum computing holds the potential to transform the way we handle credit scoring and loan evaluation. Traditional credit scoring models rely on historical data and predetermined factors to assess creditworthiness. With quantum computing, financial institutions can leverage the power of quantum algorithms to analyze a broader range of variables, including alternative data sources, social media activity, and more. This would enable more accurate and comprehensive credit assessments, ultimately leading to fairer lending practices and increased access to credit for individuals and businesses alike.

The benefits of quantum computing extend beyond traditional financial systems. One area where it could have a significant impact is in the realm of cryptocurrency and blockchain technology. Quantum computing's ability to break conventional encryption methods poses a potential threat to the security of cryptocurrencies. However, it also offers an opportunity to develop quantum-resistant encryption and blockchain algorithms that can withstand attacks from quantum computers. This would ensure the continued security and integrity of digital currencies and blockchain-based transactions.

As quantum computing continues to advance, it brings with it new challenges and considerations for the financial industry. The implementation and integration of quantum technology into existing systems would require substantial investments in infrastructure and resources. Additionally, the complexity and novelty of quantum algorithms would require financial institutions to invest in the development of quantum expertise and talent to fully harness the potential of this technology.

In conclusion, quantum computing has the power to revolutionize financial systems in ways previously unimaginable. From optimized trading strategies and advanced fraud detection to fairer credit scoring and the security of digital currencies, the applications of quantum computing in finance are vast. As the technology progresses, it is crucial for financial institutions and professionals to stay informed and adapt to the evolving landscape of quantum wealth. By embracing this technology, we have the potential to unlock new opportunities, enhance financial decision-making, and shape the future of wealth management.

Thank you for joining us on this exploration of quantum computing and its role in financial systems. We hope you have gained valuable insights into the transformative potential of quantum wealth. Stay tuned for further chapters where we will continue to delve into the fascinating world of quantum technology and its implications for the future of finance.

Chapter 4: Quantum Cryptography and Secure Transactions

In today's interconnected digital landscape, ensuring the security and privacy of financial transactions is of paramount importance. With cyber threats becoming increasingly sophisticated, the need for robust measures to safeguard against unauthorized access and data breaches has never been more critical. This is where quantum cryptography comes into play, revolutionizing the realm of secure financial transactions through the application of quantum technology.

Quantum cryptography utilizes the principles of quantum mechanics to provide an unbreakable encryption method. Unlike traditional cryptographic techniques that rely on mathematical algorithms, quantum cryptography leverages the inherent properties of quantum particles to secure communication channels. One such property, known as quantum entanglement, allows for the creation of cryptographic keys that are resistant to hacking attempts.

The use of quantum cryptography offers significant advantages over classical cryptography. One key feature is its ability to detect any tampering or eavesdropping attempts during the transmission of encrypted information. This is achieved through a unique aspect of quantum mechanics called the observer effect. Any attempt to observe or measure quantum particles in transit will inevitably alter their states, thus revealing the presence of an intruder. This ensures that secure financial transactions remain protected from potential interceptions.

Another aspect that sets quantum cryptography apart is the utilization of quantum key distribution (QKD) protocols. QKD enables the secure distribution of cryptographic keys between two parties by exploiting the principles of quantum superposition and uncertainty. By encoding information onto individual quantum particles, known as qubits, QKD guarantees that any attempt at intercepting or measuring these particles would be immediately detected, preserving the confidentiality of the cryptographic keys.

The development and implementation of quantum cryptography have led to the creation of quantum-resistant cryptographic algorithms. As the power of quantum computers continues to advance, traditional cryptographic methods face the risk of being broken by quantum algorithms. Quantum-resistant algorithms, on the other hand, are specifically designed to withstand attacks from even the most powerful quantum computers, ensuring the long-term security of financial transactions.

While the potential of quantum cryptography is vast, its practical implementation is not without challenges. The current limitations lie in the physical infrastructure required to support quantum communication networks. Building reliable and scalable quantum networks that can span large distances while maintaining the integrity of quantum signals is a complex task. Additionally, the cost associated with implementing quantum cryptography infrastructure is still relatively high, posing a barrier for widespread adoption.

Nonetheless, ongoing research and technological advancements continue to pave the way for a quantum-secured future. As quantum computers mature and quantum communication networks expand, the promise of achieving truly secure financial transactions becomes feasible. The second half of this chapter will delve into the latest developments in quantum key distribution and explore the potential impact of quantum cryptography on the financial industry. Stay tuned for the exciting revelations that await in the realm of quantum wealth and secure transactions.

Quantum Key Distribution (QKD) represents a major breakthrough in the field of quantum cryptography, offering a secure method for distributing cryptographic keys between two parties. By leveraging the principles of quantum mechanics, QKD ensures that any attempt at intercepting or measuring the quantum particles carrying the keys would be immediately detected. This revolutionary technology holds immense potential for securing financial transactions in the digital age.

One of the key advantages of QKD is its ability to provide unconditional security. Unlike classical cryptographic systems, which rely on computational complexity and the difficulty of certain mathematical problems, QKD relies on the fundamental laws of physics. The security of QKD is based on the fact that any attempt to measure a quantum particle, such as a photon, will inevitably disturb its state. This disruption can be detected by the receiving party, indicating the presence of an eavesdropper. Thus, QKD provides a robust defense against sophisticated attacks.

To ensure the successful implementation of QKD in financial transactions, several important factors must be considered. First and foremost is the need for a reliable and scalable quantum communication network. Building such a network poses significant technical challenges, as it requires the installation of secure quantum channels spanning large distances. These channels must be carefully maintained to prevent signal loss or interference, ensuring the integrity and confidentiality of quantum information. Ongoing research and development efforts are focused on overcoming these obstacles and expanding the reach of quantum communication networks.

Another critical aspect is the integration of QKD with existing financial systems and infrastructure. To fully realize the potential of quantum-secured transactions, seamless integration with banking systems, payment processors, and online platforms is essential. This requires collaboration between quantum technology experts and financial institutions to develop standardized protocols and frameworks that enable secure, interoperable transactions. Initiatives are already underway to explore the integration of QKD into existing financial systems, paving the way for a quantum-secured future.

Furthermore, the cost associated with implementing quantum cryptography infrastructure remains a challenge. Research and development efforts are focused on reducing the cost of key distribution systems and quantum communication devices to make them more accessible for widespread adoption. As technology advances and economies of scale are achieved, the costs will gradually decrease, making quantum-secured transactions more commercially viable.

The potential impact of quantum cryptography on the financial industry is far-reaching. Beyond securing transactions, quantum technology has the potential to enhance multiple areas within finance. For example, quantum computing algorithms can be utilized to optimize portfolio management, risk analysis, and asset pricing models. Moreover, secure quantum networks can enable more efficient and transparent trading platforms, reducing intermediaries and enhancing trust in the financial ecosystem.

In conclusion, the second half of this chapter has explored the immense potential of Quantum Key Distribution in securing financial transactions. By leveraging the principles of quantum mechanics, QKD provides unconditional security and offers a robust defense against cyber threats. However, the successful implementation of QKD requires the development of reliable quantum communication networks, integration with existing financial systems, and the reduction of infrastructure costs. As these challenges are addressed, the financial industry stands to benefit from the secure and transformative possibilities offered by quantum technology. The future holds exciting revelations in the realm of quantum wealth and secure transactions, revolutionizing the way we conduct and safeguard financial exchanges.

Chapter 5: Quantum Algorithms for Financial Modeling

Quantum technology has the potential to revolutionize various industries, and finance is no exception. In recent years, researchers and experts have begun exploring the use of quantum algorithms in financial modeling to unlock new levels of accuracy and predictive power. This exciting development holds immense promise for investors, economists, and financial analysts seeking a competitive edge in the world of finance.

Financial modeling is a crucial aspect of decision-making in the financial realm. It involves creating mathematical representations of real-world financial situations, enabling professionals to understand and predict market trends, assess risk, and make informed investment choices. However, traditional financial modeling approaches have their limitations. Complex financial systems, influenced by numerous factors, can be challenging to capture accurately through conventional calculations.

This is where quantum algorithms step in as a potential game-changer. Quantum computers harness the laws of quantum mechanics to process vast amounts of information simultaneously, offering the potential for exponentially faster calculations. These quantum algorithms have the ability to solve problems that would be practically impossible or exceedingly time-consuming for classical computers.

One quantum algorithm that shows promise in financial modeling is the quantum Fourier transform (QFT). By leveraging the principles of quantum superposition and entanglement, the QFT allows for the efficient analysis of periodic patterns in financial data. This can prove invaluable when analyzing time-series data, such as stock prices and market trends, where identifying hidden patterns can lead to more accurate predictions.

Additionally, quantum algorithms like the quantum approximate optimization algorithm (QAOA) hold promise for portfolio optimization. Portfolio optimization involves finding the optimal allocation of assets to maximize returns while minimizing risk. Traditional approaches to portfolio optimization can be computationally intensive and may provide suboptimal solutions due to simplifying assumptions. The QAOA, powered by quantum computers, offers the potential to tackle this complex optimization problem more efficiently.

Furthermore, quantum machine learning algorithms, such as quantum support vector machines (QSVM) and quantum neural networks (QNN), open new avenues for financial modeling. These algorithms harness quantum computational power to process and analyze vast amounts of financial data, enabling enhanced pattern recognition and more accurate predictions.

By incorporating quantum algorithms into financial modeling, researchers and practitioners aim to unlock new insights and predictions, leading to smarter investment strategies and risk assessments. This amalgamation of quantum technology and finance has the potential to revolutionize the way financial decisions are made, offering a more accurate representation of the dynamic and complex nature of financial markets.

As we delve deeper into the realm of quantum algorithms for financial modeling, we will explore various algorithms, their applications, and their impact on risk assessment, portfolio optimization, and predictive modeling. In the second half of this chapter, we will showcase real-world examples and delve into the potential challenges and ethical considerations surrounding the integration of quantum algorithms into the financial industry. Brace yourself for an in-depth journey into the fascinating world of quantum-driven financial modeling.Quantum algorithms have emerged as a powerful tool in financial modeling, offering new possibilities to enhance risk assessment, portfolio optimization, and predictive modeling. As we delve deeper into the amalgamation of quantum technology and finance, it is essential to examine real-world examples, understand the potential challenges, and explore the ethical considerations surrounding the integration of quantum algorithms into the financial industry.

One practical application of quantum algorithms in financial modeling is risk assessment. Traditional approaches often rely on simplified assumptions and historical patterns, which may not capture the dynamic and complex nature of markets accurately. However, quantum machine learning algorithms, such as quantum support vector machines (QSVM) and quantum neural networks (QNN), can process vast amounts of financial data in parallel, enabling enhanced pattern recognition and more accurate risk assessment.

By harnessing the power of quantum computing, analysts can train quantum algorithms on large datasets to identify subtle correlations, hidden patterns, and interdependencies between market variables. These insights can significantly improve risk models, providing a more comprehensive understanding of market fluctuations and potential downside risks.

Moreover, portfolio optimization is a critical area where quantum algorithms can make a significant impact. Traditional approaches often struggle to balance risk and return across multiple assets accurately. Computationally intensive methods that consider various constraints can still yield suboptimal results due to the sheer complexity of the problem.

Quantum approximate optimization algorithm (QAOA) provides a promising solution to this puzzle. By leveraging the capabilities of quantum computing, the QAOA can efficiently solve complex optimization problems by exploring a superposition of potential solutions. This approach enables analysts to identify the optimal asset allocation that maximizes returns while minimizing risk, taking into account various constraints and objectives simultaneously.

Real-world examples have already showcased the power of quantum algorithms in portfolio optimization. For instance, a study conducted by researchers at the University of Waterloo used the QAOA to optimize an investment portfolio with 16 assets. The results demonstrated that the quantum algorithm outperformed traditional approaches in terms of risk-adjusted returns, providing a valuable tool for asset managers seeking to optimize their portfolios in a rapidly changing market.

While the integration of quantum algorithms into finance brings immense potential, it is crucial to address the associated challenges. Quantum computers are still in the early stages of development, with limited qubits and susceptibility to noise and errors. As the technology progresses, these limitations are expected to be overcome, but for now, it poses practical limitations on implementing quantum algorithms for financial modeling.

Additionally, ethical considerations must be taken into account. The use of quantum algorithms in finance raises concerns about the potential for unfair advantages or market manipulation. Regulators and industry participants must collaborate to establish guidelines and safeguard against the misuse of this powerful technology.

In conclusion, the integration of quantum algorithms in financial modeling brings exciting possibilities for enhanced accuracy and predictive power. Risk assessment, portfolio optimization, and predictive modeling are areas where quantum algorithms have showcased significant potential. Real-world examples highlight the superiority of quantum algorithms in optimizing portfolios and improving risk models. However, it is important to address the challenges of quantum computing's early stages and understand the ethical implications associated with its application in finance. As quantum technology continues to advance, the fascinating world of quantum-driven financial modeling promises to revolutionize the way financial decisions are made. The promise of unlocking new insights and predictions opens doors to smarter investment strategies and more accurate representations of complex financial markets.

Chapter 6: Quantum Machine Learning for Investment Strategies

Investigating how quantum machine learning is revolutionizing investment strategies and portfolio management.

In recent years, the field of quantum machine learning has emerged as a promising area of research, poised to revolutionize the financial industry. As the world becomes increasingly complex and interconnected, traditional investment strategies struggle to keep up with the pace of change. This is where quantum technology comes into play, offering a new frontier for investors seeking to unlock untapped financial potential.

Quantum machine learning combines the power of quantum computing and artificial intelligence to identify complex patterns and make informed investment decisions. By harnessing the principles of quantum mechanics, these machines are capable of processing vast amounts of data and solving problems that are beyond the reach of classical computers. This breakthrough technology has the potential to transform investment strategies and redefine portfolio management.

One of the key advantages of quantum machine learning is its ability to analyze data in multiple dimensions simultaneously. Traditional machine learning algorithms require simplification and dimensionality reduction, often resulting in the loss of important information. Quantum machine learning, on the other hand, leverages the inherent parallelism of quantum computing to extract meaningful insights from high-dimensional datasets without sacrificing accuracy.

By applying quantum algorithms to financial data, investors can uncover hidden patterns and correlations that were previously undetectable. This enables more accurate predictions of market trends, risk assessment, and the optimization of investment portfolios. Quantum machine learning algorithms excel at finding non-linear relationships and capturing subtle market dynamics that can greatly influence investment outcomes.

Moreover, quantum machine learning algorithms inherently have the ability to adapt to changing market conditions in real-time. The flexibility and adaptability of these algorithms allow investors to react swiftly to market fluctuations, seize opportunities, and minimize risks. This dynamic approach to investment strategies offers a competitive edge in increasingly volatile and uncertain markets.

While the potential of quantum machine learning for investment strategies is promising, there are still significant challenges to overcome. The implementation of quantum technology in finance requires a deep understanding of both quantum mechanics and finance, as well as substantial computational resources. Additionally, the development of quantum-safe encryption techniques is crucial to ensure the security of sensitive financial data.

Despite these challenges, quantum machine learning represents an exciting frontier in the world of finance. As researchers continue to advance the field, we can anticipate the development of more sophisticated algorithms and increased adoption of quantum technology in investment strategies.

In the second half of this chapter, we will delve deeper into the specific applications of quantum machine learning in investment strategies. We will explore how it can improve risk assessment, optimize portfolio diversification, and enhance market forecasting. Prepare to immerse yourself in the fascinating world of quantum-driven finance, where technology meets wealth creation. Stay tuned for the surprising revelations in the next part of this chapter.In the second half of this chapter, we will explore the specific applications of quantum machine learning in investment strategies. By harnessing the power of quantum technology, investors can enhance their risk assessment capabilities, optimize portfolio diversification, and improve market forecasting.

One of the key challenges in investment strategies is accurately assessing and managing risk. Traditional risk assessment models rely on historical data and assumptions about the relationships between different assets. However, these models often fail to capture the complexities and interdependencies of today's financial markets. Quantum machine learning offers a novel approach to risk assessment by leveraging quantum algorithms to analyze data in multiple dimensions simultaneously. This enables investors to uncover hidden patterns and correlations that were previously undetectable, leading to more accurate risk assessments.

With the ability to process vast amounts of data and identify complex patterns, quantum machine learning can optimize portfolio diversification. Diversification is a fundamental strategy used to spread investments across different asset classes and reduce risk. However, finding the optimal allocation across diverse assets can be challenging. Quantum machine learning algorithms can consider multiple factors simultaneously, such as asset performance, correlations, and market trends, to determine the most effective asset allocation strategy. This can lead to improved portfolio performance and better risk management.

Market forecasting is another area where quantum machine learning can provide significant advantages. Accurately predicting market trends is crucial for successful investment strategies. Traditional forecasting models often rely on linear relationships and assumptions that may not hold true in complex financial markets. Quantum machine learning, with its ability to capture non-linear relationships and subtle market dynamics, can provide more accurate and reliable market forecasts. This can enable investors to make informed decisions, seize opportunities, and stay ahead of market fluctuations.

Moreover, the flexibility and adaptability of quantum machine learning algorithms offer a competitive edge in volatile and uncertain markets. Quantum algorithms can adapt to changing market conditions in real-time, allowing investors to swiftly adjust their strategies, seize emerging opportunities, and minimize risks. In today's fast-paced financial landscape, the ability to quickly respond and adapt to market dynamics is crucial for success.

While the potential of quantum machine learning for investment strategies is exciting, it is important to acknowledge the challenges that come with its implementation. Quantum technology requires a deep understanding of both quantum mechanics and finance, as well as significant computational resources. Additionally, ensuring the security of sensitive financial data through the development of quantum-safe encryption techniques is crucial.

In conclusion, quantum machine learning has the potential to revolutionize investment strategies and portfolio management. By leveraging the power of quantum computing and artificial intelligence, investors can unlock untapped financial potential, make more accurate predictions, optimize portfolio diversification, and improve risk management. While there are challenges to overcome, the continued advancement of the field holds promising prospects for the adoption and refinement of quantum-driven finance. As we delve deeper into this fascinating world, we witness the convergence of technology and wealth creation, where quantum machine learning opens doors to new possibilities in the financial industry. Stay tuned for the surprising revelations that lie ahead.

Chapter 7: Quantum Sensor Technologies in Financial Markets

In today's fast-paced and ever-changing financial landscape, the ability to analyze and interpret market data with speed and accuracy is paramount. To unlock the full potential of financial markets, innovative technologies have emerged, and one technology in particular has gained significant attention: quantum sensor technologies. Combining the principles of quantum mechanics with data analysis, these technologies have revolutionized the way we understand and navigate the complex world of finance.

At its core, quantum sensor technology harnesses the unique properties of quantum mechanics to measure and analyze a variety of financial parameters. These sensors exhibit remarkable sensitivity, allowing for precise measurements of market variables such as price fluctuations, trading volumes, and risk evaluations. By providing a more detailed and nuanced picture of the financial landscape, quantum sensors enable traders, investors, and financial institutions to make more informed decisions.

The use of quantum sensor technologies in financial markets offers several distinct advantages. Firstly, their sensitivity allows for the detection of subtle changes in market conditions that might otherwise go unnoticed. This enables traders to identify emerging trends, detect anomalies, and respond swiftly to market shifts. By leveraging these insights, investors can potentially increase their profits and mitigate risks.

Additionally, quantum sensors provide real-time data with unparalleled accuracy. Traditional financial analysis tools often rely on historical data, which may not capture the most up-to-date market dynamics. By contrast, quantum sensors continuously gather and process data in real-time, providing a comprehensive and dynamic view of the financial landscape. This empowers investors to adapt quickly to changing market conditions and seize opportunities as they arise.

Moreover, the speed at which quantum sensors operate is truly remarkable. Utilizing the principles of quantum entanglement and superposition, these sensors can perform complex calculations exponentially faster than classical computers. This enables financial institutions to process vast amounts of data in a fraction of the time it would take with traditional methods. Consequently, traders can make split-second decisions with greater confidence, potentially gaining an edge over competitors.

In addition to their speed and accuracy, quantum sensors bring enhanced security to financial markets. With the rise of digital transactions and the increasing sophistication of cyber threats, the ability to protect sensitive financial information is of utmost importance. Quantum sensor technologies offer a level of security that is inherently robust due to their reliance on quantum principles. The encryption algorithms built upon quantum mechanics are fundamentally unbreakable, safeguarding financial data and ensuring the integrity of transactions.

As quantum sensor technologies continue to evolve, their impact on financial markets is poised to be transformative. The ability to analyze market data with unparalleled speed, precision, and security opens up new avenues for wealth generation and risk management. In the second half of this chapter, we will explore specific applications of quantum sensors in different financial sectors and delve deeper into their potential implications. Join us as we unveil the exciting possibilities that lie ahead and unlock the true power of quantum wealth.In the second half of this chapter, we will explore specific applications of quantum sensor technologies in different financial sectors and delve even deeper into their potential implications. By understanding these applications, we can begin to grasp the immense possibilities that lie ahead and unlock the true power of quantum wealth.

One notable area where quantum sensors are making waves is in high-frequency trading (HFT). HFT relies on split-second decision-making and requires real-time data to capitalize on market fluctuations. Quantum sensors' ability to process vast amounts of data at an unprecedented speed makes them particularly well-suited for this field. By providing traders with up-to-the-minute market insights, quantum sensors enable them to execute trades rapidly and gain a competitive edge.

Moreover, in the field of risk management, the application of quantum sensor technologies has proven invaluable. Traditional risk models often rely on historical data and can struggle to account for unforeseen events or unprecedented market conditions. Quantum sensors, with their real-time data and nuanced understanding of market variables, offer a more accurate and dynamic assessment of risk. Financial institutions can leverage this information to make informed decisions and navigate potential pitfalls with greater confidence.

Furthermore, quantum sensors are also revolutionizing portfolio optimization techniques. Asset managers and investors rely on portfolio optimization strategies to maximize returns while minimizing risk. The inclusion of quantum sensors allows for a more comprehensive evaluation of assets, taking into consideration the interconnectedness and complexity of the financial landscape. By providing a more accurate assessment of asset correlations and risk exposures, quantum sensors aid in constructing optimized portfolios that withstand market volatility.

In addition to these applications, quantum sensor technologies are proving instrumental in the field of fraud detection and prevention. With the rise of sophisticated financial crimes, including identity theft and money laundering, it is crucial to have robust systems in place to safeguard against these threats. Quantum sensors, with their enhanced security features built upon the principles of quantum mechanics, offer a formidable defense against cyber attacks. The inherent computational complexity of quantum sensors makes it nearly impossible for malicious actors to compromise financial systems and exploit vulnerabilities.

As the development of quantum sensor technologies progresses, there are exciting possibilities on the horizon. Financial markets stand to benefit from enhanced speed, accuracy, security, and risk management capabilities enabled by quantum sensors. However, it is important to acknowledge that there are still challenges to overcome, such as scalability and cost-effectiveness. The integration of quantum sensors into existing financial infrastructures will require innovative solutions and collaboration between the scientific and financial communities.

In conclusion, quantum sensor technologies are ushering in a new era of financial analysis and decision-making. Through their unparalleled speed, accuracy, and security, quantum sensors empower traders, investors, and financial institutions to make more informed choices. Exciting applications in high-frequency trading, risk management, portfolio optimization, and fraud prevention demonstrate the potential for quantum sensors to reshape financial markets. It is crucial for individuals and organizations in the financial industry to stay abreast of these developments and embrace the possibilities offered by quantum wealth. As we look ahead, the path to unlocking the full potential of quantum sensor technologies in financial markets promises to be transformative.

Chapter 8: Quantum Communication for Financial Networks

In the rapidly evolving landscape of technology, quantum communication has emerged as a disruptive force, revolutionizing industries across the board. Among the myriad sectors benefiting from this groundbreaking technology is the world of finance. In this chapter, we delve into the realm of quantum communication and its potential to establish secure and efficient financial networks, propelling us further into the era of quantum wealth.

Before we explore the benefits, it is crucial to understand the fundamental principles underlying quantum communication. Unlike classical communication, which relies on transmitting information through electrical impulses, quantum communication employs the principles of quantum mechanics to ensure unparalleled security and reliability.

One of the key advantages of quantum communication lies in its ability to provide secure transmission of financial data. Through a phenomenon known as quantum key distribution (QKD), information can be exchanged in a manner that is impervious to interception or eavesdropping. This is made possible by utilizing the properties of quantum particles, such as photons, which are inherently sensitive to any attempt at observation or measurement.

By employing QKD protocols, financial institutions can establish communication channels that guarantee the confidentiality and integrity of sensitive data, including transactions, account details, and personal information. This enhanced security mitigates the risk of cyber-attacks and fraud, instilling trust in the financial network and providing peace of mind to both businesses and individuals.

Furthermore, quantum communication has the potential to vastly improve the efficiency of financial networks. Traditional communication systems often experience bottlenecks due to the limitations of transmitting vast amounts of data over long distances. However, quantum communication offers a solution to this challenge through a phenomenon known as entanglement.

Entanglement allows for the instantaneous transfer of information, regardless of the physical distance between quantum particles. Through entanglement-based protocols, financial transactions could be executed seamlessly across global networks, eliminating the need for intermediaries and reducing transaction times to near-instantaneous speeds. This not only streamlines the financial process but also opens up new avenues for international collaborations and markets.

Moreover, the utilization of quantum communication in financial networks enables greater scalability. As the demand for financial services continues to grow, traditional systems face challenges in handling the increasing load and complexity. In contrast, quantum communication has the potential to scale efficiently, overcoming these limitations. By leveraging the unique properties of quantum particles, such as superposition and entanglement, financial networks can expand without sacrificing security or efficiency.

As we begin to realize the full potential of quantum communication in establishing secure and efficient financial networks, we are on the cusp of a quantum wealth revolution. The harnessing of quantum technology has the power to reshape the way we conduct financial transactions, ensuring a future that is not only secure but also expedient and globally interconnected.

Stay tuned for the second half of this chapter, where we explore the practical applications and future implications of quantum communication in the realm of financial networks. The possibilities are groundbreaking, and the next steps towards a quantum-powered financial landscape will change the way we perceive and engage with wealth.As we continue our exploration of quantum communication for financial networks, let us delve into the practical applications and future implications of this groundbreaking technology. The capabilities offered by quantum communication are truly transformative, paving the way for an era of unprecedented financial potential.

One of the most promising applications of quantum communication in the financial realm is secure quantum messaging. Traditional messaging systems are vulnerable to attacks, with cybercriminals exploiting weaknesses for their nefarious purposes. However, by harnessing the power of quantum mechanics, quantum messaging ensures a communication channel that is truly secure and tamper-proof.

Through the use of quantum information carriers, such as entangled photons or qubits, financial institutions can exchange messages that are impossible to intercept without detection. The secure transmission of information allows for the authentication, verification, and integrity of messages, safeguarding vital financial data from unauthorized access.

Furthermore, quantum communication opens up exciting possibilities for decentralized financial systems. With the rise of cryptocurrencies and blockchain technology, quantum communication can address critical security concerns surrounding digital assets. Quantum-resistant encryption algorithms can protect the cryptographic keys that secure digital currencies, making them impervious to attacks by quantum computers.

Moreover, the inherent scalability of quantum communication enables the seamless integration of decentralized finance (DeFi) platforms. By leveraging the power of quantum computing, DeFi systems can handle complex computations and transactions with unmatched speed and efficiency, making them ideal for tasks such as smart contract execution, asset management, and decentralized exchanges.

In addition to revolutionizing the security and decentralized nature of financial networks, quantum communication also plays a pivotal role in enhancing financial data analysis. Traditional financial analytics often involve time-consuming computations and data processing. However, with the advent of quantum computing, complex financial algorithms can be executed at a significantly accelerated pace.

The ability of quantum computers to perform parallel calculations and solve complex optimization problems allows for more accurate risk assessment, asset allocation, and predictive modeling. Financial institutions can harness the power of quantum computing to gain deeper insights into market trends, improve investment strategies, and identify new opportunities for growth and profitability.

Looking ahead, the future implications of quantum communication in financial networks are vast and far-reaching. Quantum technology holds incredible potential to revolutionize not only the way we conduct financial transactions but also the very nature of money itself.

In the era of quantum wealth, financial networks will be seamlessly interconnected, facilitating rapid and secure transactions across borders. The integration of quantum communication in international banking systems will promote global collaboration and economic growth, eliminating barriers and inefficiencies that currently hinder cross-border transactions.

Moreover, the increased efficiency and security offered by quantum communication will foster a climate of trust and transparency within the financial industry. Individuals and businesses alike will have peace of mind, knowing that their financial transactions and assets are protected by unbreakable quantum encryption.

As we close this chapter on quantum communication for financial networks, it is clear that the potential of this technology is staggering. The era of quantum wealth is upon us, and the boundaries of what we can achieve in the realm of finance are expanding exponentially.

Keep your eyes peeled for the next chapter, where we venture into the realm of quantum computing and its transformative impact on financial modeling and artificial intelligence. Together, we embark on an extraordinary journey towards a future where quantum technology reshapes the very fabric of financial systems.

Chapter 9: Quantum Simulations and Risk Analysis

Quantum technology has been revolutionizing various fields, and the financial world is no exception. In this chapter, we delve into the fascinating realm of quantum simulations and their ability to enhance risk analysis, ultimately leading to better decision-making in financial contexts.

Traditionally, risk analysis in finance has relied on numerical models and simulations that attempt to capture the complex interplay of various factors. However, these conventional methods often struggle to accurately represent the intricate nature of financial systems. This is where quantum simulations offer a promising alternative.

Quantum simulations utilize the principles of quantum mechanics to explore and simulate complex systems with unprecedented speed and accuracy. By harnessing the power of quantum computers, which operate on quantum bits (qubits) instead of classical bits, financial analysts can gain deeper insights into the potential risks associated with various investment strategies.

One key advantage of quantum simulations lies in their ability to handle large-scale calculations efficiently. Classical computers face limitations when managing numerous variables simultaneously, but quantum computers excel in handling vast amounts of data and complex calculations. This empowers analysts to model intricate financial systems more accurately, resulting in a more sophisticated understanding of potential risks.

In risk analysis, precise predictions are vital for making informed decisions. Quantum simulations enable researchers to explore a wide range of scenarios by simulating different market conditions and investment strategies. This comprehensive analysis provides invaluable insights into the potential outcomes and associated risk levels, allowing investors to mitigate their exposure to potential losses.

Moreover, the inherent nature of quantum systems offers enhanced speed and parallelism, enabling quantum simulations to explore a multitude of scenarios in a shorter time frame. This acceleration in computational capabilities expedites the risk analysis process, providing decision-makers with real-time information and agility in adapting investment plans.

Another exciting aspect of quantum simulations is their unique capacity to factor in quantum phenomena, such as entanglement and superposition, that influence financial systems. These quantum effects can have a profound impact on risk analysis, as they allow for a more holistic understanding of the interconnectedness within financial markets. By considering these quantum phenomena, analysts can identify potential correlations and patterns that may not be evident in classical simulations.

As we move forward, the integration of quantum simulations into risk analysis holds immense potential for the financial sector. Through a combination of increased computational power, enhanced accuracy, and the ability to consider quantum phenomena, analysts can gain deeper insights into the complexities of financial markets. This improved understanding empowers decision-makers with more robust risk assessments, ultimately facilitating better-informed investment strategies.

Quantum simulations represent an exciting frontier in financial risk analysis, opening up new avenues for investors and analysts alike. In the second half of this chapter, we will explore specific applications of quantum simulations in mitigating risk, from portfolio optimization to asset pricing. Prepare to dive deeper into the realm of quantum technology and witness its transformative impact on financial decision-making.

(End of the first half of the chapter)The first half of this chapter explored the immense potential of quantum simulations in improving risk analysis and decision-making in the financial world. We delved into the advantages of quantum simulations, such as their ability to handle large-scale calculations efficiently, their capacity to factor in quantum phenomena, and their enhanced speed and parallelism. These features provide financial analysts with invaluable insights into complex financial systems, empowering them to make informed investment strategies.

Now, let us dive deeper into the specific applications of quantum simulations in mitigating risk and enhancing financial decision-making. One significant area where quantum simulations prove instrumental is portfolio optimization. In traditional finance, optimizing portfolios is a challenging task due to the vast number of potential asset combinations and their dynamic interactions. However, quantum simulations offer a way to explore and analyze these combinations more comprehensively and efficiently.

By leveraging the computational power of quantum computers, analysts can generate a vast number of simulations to identify optimal asset allocations. These simulations consider various factors such as historical performance, risk profiles, and market trends. The ability to handle large-scale calculations and factor in the interconnectedness of financial markets allows for the identification of well-diversified portfolios with minimal risk exposure.

Furthermore, quantum simulations enable analysts to conduct stress tests on portfolios, subjecting them to various economic scenarios and market shocks. This stress-testing process helps identify vulnerabilities and potential risk factors, allowing investors to make adjustments to their portfolios accordingly. By incorporating quantum simulations into portfolio optimization, investors can make more robust and resilient investment strategies.

Another application of quantum simulations in risk analysis is asset pricing. Valuing financial assets accurately is crucial for investors and financial institutions. Traditional pricing models often rely on simplifying assumptions that fail to capture the intricate dynamics and complexities of financial markets. Quantum simulations, on the other hand, provide a more accurate representation of these dynamics by considering quantum phenomena and interconnections.

With the assistance of quantum simulations, analysts can generate real-time pricing models that account for the impact of various factors, such as interest rates, market volatility, and macroeconomic indicators. By analyzing vast amounts of data and running simulations, analysts can determine the fair value of financial assets more accurately, reducing the potential for mispricing and improving investment decision-making.

Furthermore, quantum simulations offer the potential to explore the pricing of derivative assets more effectively. Derivatives, such as options and futures contracts, derive their value from underlying assets. However, accurately pricing derivatives is a complex task due to their nonlinear nature and high-dimensional risk factors. Quantum simulations can enhance derivative pricing models by incorporating a more comprehensive understanding of financial systems, leading to improved valuations and risk assessments.

In conclusion, the integration of quantum simulations into risk analysis and financial decision-making opens up new avenues for investors and analysts. The second half of this chapter focused on two specific applications of quantum simulations: portfolio optimization and asset pricing. By leveraging the features of quantum simulations, such as their ability to handle vast amounts of data, factor in quantum phenomena, and consider interconnections within financial markets, analysts can make more informed investment decisions and mitigate risks effectively.

As we continue exploring the transformative impact of quantum technology on financial decision-making, the possibilities for unlocking financial potential with quantum wealth become even more exciting. Stay tuned for more insights into the fascinating world of quantum simulations and their role in revolutionizing the financial sector.

Chapter 10: Quantum-Based Wealth Management Strategies

Introduction

In an evolving world where technology constantly pushes the boundaries of what is possible, the realm of wealth management has found itself at the forefront of innovation. Traditional approaches are being augmented by emerging technologies, and one such groundbreaking field making waves is quantum technology. By harnessing the power of quantum mechanics, wealth management strategies are taking a giant leap forward, promising increased financial prosperity for those who dare to embrace this quantum revolution.

Understanding the Quantum Realm

To comprehend the potential of quantum-based wealth management strategies, one must first grasp the fundamental principles of quantum mechanics. Unlike classical physics, quantum mechanics explores the behavior of matter and energy at tiny, subatomic scales. It reveals that particles such as electrons can exist in multiple states simultaneously, a concept known as superposition, fundamentally defying the classical notion of binary choices.

Quantum Computing in Wealth Management

Traditional wealth management strategies have often relied on complex mathematical models and empirical data analysis to optimize investment decisions. However, the processing power of classical computers has imposed limitations on their effectiveness. Enter quantum computing, a paradigm-shifting technology capable of processing vast amounts of data exponentially faster than traditional computers.

By leveraging the inherent parallelism and superposition of quantum bits, or qubits, quantum computers have the potential to solve complex problems that were previously intractable. In the world of wealth management, this means quantum algorithms can efficiently analyze vast financial datasets, identify hidden patterns, and make near-instantaneous investment recommendations with unparalleled accuracy.

Quantum encryption and data security

As the financial sector becomes increasingly digitized, data security concerns become paramount. Quantum cryptography, an application of quantum physics, offers a novel solution. Traditional cryptographic systems rely on computational complexity to secure information, but quantum encryption leverages the fundamental principles of quantum mechanics to provide a level of security that surpasses classical methods.

Quantum key distribution (QKD) is a leading example of quantum encryption, where the transmission of encryption keys using quantum states ensures secure communication channels. Quantum technologies make eavesdropping nearly impossible due to the inherent uncertainty principle, strengthening the trust in financial transactions while mitigating the risks of cyberattacks and data breaches.

Quantum Machine Learning in Wealth Management

Machine learning algorithms play a crucial role in wealth management by automating decision-making processes and enhancing investment strategies. Quantum machine learning (QML) takes these capabilities to new heights by integrating the power of quantum computing with the intelligence of machine learning.

By leveraging quantum computing's ability to process complex and interconnected datasets, quantum machine learning algorithms can uncover valuable insights from financial markets that were previously hidden. QML models can adapt and evolve, learning from market dynamics, economic indicators, and even social sentiment. This promises to revolutionize portfolio optimization, risk management, and market forecasting, ultimately leading to better financial outcomes for investors.

Conclusion

The first half of this chapter has delved into the exciting realm of quantum-based wealth management strategies. We've explored the principles of quantum mechanics, seen how quantum computing can revolutionize investment decision-making, and how quantum encryption and quantum machine learning can ensure the security and efficiency of financial transactions. Stay tuned for the second half of the chapter, where we will unravel the potential applications and future implications of this fascinating field.Exploring Quantum-Based Wealth Management Strategies

In the previous section, we established a foundation of understanding for quantum-based wealth management strategies. Now, let's dive deeper into the potential applications and future implications of this fascinating field.

Quantum Risk Analysis and Portfolios Optimization

One of the key areas where quantum technology can revolutionize wealth management is risk analysis and portfolio optimization. Traditional methods often rely on mean-variance optimization techniques to construct investment portfolios. However, these approaches struggle to account for the complexity and interconnectedness of modern financial markets.

Quantum computing offers a solution to this problem by providing the computational power to optimize portfolios on a magnitude previously unattainable. By examining multiple states simultaneously and analyzing vast datasets, quantum algorithms can consider an extensive range of parameters, market dynamics, and economic indicators. This enables them to identify optimal portfolio compositions that maximize returns and minimize risks, leading to better financial outcomes for investors.

Furthermore, quantum-based risk analysis models are not limited to traditional financial data. They can also incorporate non-traditional sources such as social sentiment analysis, news sentiment, and even alternative data sets like weather patterns or satellite imagery. By expanding the array of inputs and considering a more comprehensive risk assessment, quantum-powered strategies offer a nuanced and robust approach to portfolio management.

Quantum-Based Market Forecasting

Accurate market forecasting is a critical aspect of wealth management. Traditional methods often rely on historical data and statistical models to predict market trends. While these approaches can be valuable, they have their limitations, particularly in capturing instantaneous market dynamics and unforeseen events.

Quantum machine learning (QML) algorithms bring a new level of sophistication to market forecasting. By analyzing vast amounts of real-time data from multiple sources, including social media, news, and financial data streams, QML models can identify hidden patterns and correlations that traditional methods often miss.

Furthermore, quantum computing's ability to process interconnected datasets in parallel allows QML algorithms to adapt and evolve as market conditions change. By continuously learning from new information and adjusting their predictions, quantum-based market forecasting strategies provide investors with more accurate insights, helping them make informed and timely investment decisions.

Quantum Ethics and Regulatory Challenges

While the potential benefits of quantum-based wealth management strategies are vast, they are not without ethical and regulatory challenges. As these technologies continue to advance, ensuring responsible and equitable use becomes paramount.

The integration of quantum computing and machine learning in wealth management brings to the forefront concerns regarding algorithmic bias, data security, and privacy. It is crucial for financial institutions and policymakers to establish robust frameworks and regulations that address these issues, ensuring that financial technologies are used responsibly and in the best interest of all stakeholders.

Conclusion

In conclusion, quantum-based wealth management strategies are poised to disrupt and transform the financial industry. From optimizing portfolios and risk analysis to market forecasting, quantum technology offers unprecedented computational power and analytical capabilities.

However, harnessing the potential of quantum wealth management will require careful consideration of ethical implications and regulatory frameworks. As this field progresses, it is vital for industry experts, policymakers, and investors to collaborate and address these challenges to ensure the realization of a quantum revolution that benefits everyone.

This chapter has provided an overview of quantum-based wealth management strategies, from understanding the principles of quantum mechanics to exploring the applications and implications in financial decision-making. By embracing the opportunities presented by quantum technology, investors can unlock new levels of financial prosperity.

Chapter 11: Ethical Considerations and Quantum Finance

As the world continues to progress and evolve, technological advancements have consistently played a significant role in shaping various aspects of our lives. One such area that has witnessed exponential growth and transformation is the financial sector. With the emergence of quantum technology, a new frontier in finance has opened, presenting both promising opportunities and ethical considerations.

Quantum finance, at its core, harnesses the power of quantum algorithms and computations to optimize investment strategies, risk management, and portfolio analysis. By utilizing the principles of quantum mechanics, such as superposition and entanglement, financial institutions are exploring innovative ways to improve decision-making processes and maximize returns. However, this growing intersection between quantum technology and finance necessitates a deeper examination of the ethical implications it carries.

One key ethical consideration in quantum finance revolves around data privacy and security. The vast amounts of sensitive financial information processed through quantum algorithms raise concerns over safeguarding individuals' personal and transactional data. As quantum computing holds the potential to break current encryption methods, there is a need for robust privacy frameworks and encryption techniques to protect against potential breaches. Striking a delicate balance between utilizing powerful quantum technologies while upholding individual privacy rights is vital for maintaining societal trust.

Another significant ethical concern lies in the potential exacerbation of existing financial inequalities. The implementation of quantum finance strategies may disproportionately benefit those with greater access to quantum technology and computational resources. Without adequate regulatory safeguards and ethical guidelines, a digital divide could deepen, further marginalizing already vulnerable populations. Therefore, it becomes imperative to foster inclusivity in the quantum finance landscape and ensure equitable distribution of its benefits.

Moreover, the influence of quantum finance on traditional financial markets raises questions of fair competition. With the integration of quantum algorithms in high-frequency trading and asset pricing, concerns arise regarding market manipulation and the integrity of price discovery. Regulatory bodies must carefully monitor and assess the impact of quantum finance to prevent monopolistic practices and maintain a level playing field for all participants. Transparency and adherence to ethical principles should be at the forefront of this evolving financial landscape.

Furthermore, the potential consequences of erroneous quantum-based financial decision-making cannot be overlooked. The inherent complexity of quantum algorithms, coupled with the uncertainty surrounding quantum systems, introduces an element of unpredictability and potential systemic risk. Ensuring accountability and responsible use of quantum finance tools is crucial to mitigate the potential harm that can arise from flawed or poorly implemented strategies.

In conclusion, the emergence of quantum finance brings forth a multitude of ethical considerations that must be thoroughly examined. As algorithms and computations continue to shape our financial systems, prioritizing data privacy, fostering inclusivity, promoting fairness, and maintaining accountability will be paramount. Striking a delicate balance between the potential benefits of quantum technology and societal well-being will be a vital challenge for policymakers, financial institutions, and stakeholders alike.

(End of the first half of Chapter 11)With the rapid development of quantum technology in the financial sector, it is essential to recognize and address the ethical considerations that come along with it. In the second half of this chapter, we will delve deeper into two significant ethical concerns surrounding quantum finance – algorithmic bias and the potential impact on job displacement.

Algorithmic bias, though not exclusive to quantum finance, remains a critical ethical issue in the application of any computational technology. As quantum algorithms continue to advance and shape financial decision-making processes, it is essential to ensure that these algorithms are not prone to biases that may perpetuate discrimination or negatively affect certain societal groups.

Quantum algorithms, like their classical counterparts, rely on massive datasets to derive insights and make predictions. However, if these datasets are incomplete, biased, or reflect discriminatory patterns, the resulting algorithms may reinforce these biases, leading to unfair treatment or exclusion in financial transactions.

To mitigate algorithmic bias, it is crucial to develop robust and transparent frameworks for auditing and assessing the fairness of quantum algorithms. This involves examining the datasets used during algorithm training to identify any biases present and taking appropriate steps to address them. Additionally, involving diverse groups of experts in the design and development of quantum algorithms can help account for different perspectives, thereby reducing the risk of bias.

Another ethical concern associated with quantum finance is the potential impact on job displacement. As quantum technology progresses, it holds the potential to streamline and automate various financial processes, potentially leading to the elimination of certain job roles. This can pose significant challenges, especially for individuals who rely on these jobs for their livelihoods.

To address this concern, proactive measures must be taken by both policymakers and financial institutions. Providing reskilling and upskilling opportunities for individuals at risk of job displacement is crucial to ensure a smooth transition into new roles within the evolving quantum finance landscape. Moreover, fostering innovation and entrepreneurship in areas that complement quantum finance, such as quantum technology development or data analysis, can create new employment opportunities and drive economic growth.

Additionally, it is vital to recognize that while quantum technology may automate certain tasks, it also has the potential to create new job roles and opportunities that harness the power of this emerging technology. By actively promoting education and training programs focused on quantum technologies, individuals can gain the skills required to thrive in this transformative era of finance.

In conclusion, as quantum finance continues to advance, it is essential to address the ethical considerations surrounding algorithmic bias and job displacement. By prioritizing fairness and inclusivity in algorithm design and implementation, and by implementing proactive measures to mitigate job displacement, we can strive to create a quantum finance landscape that positively impacts both financial outcomes and societal well-being.

The collaboration and cooperation of policymakers, financial institutions, and stakeholders will be crucial in navigating the ethical dimensions of quantum finance. By remaining vigilant and committed to upholding ethical principles, we can unlock the full potential of quantum technology while ensuring its benefits are harnessed in a responsible and inclusive manner.

As we move forward, it is imperative to continue the dialogue around ethical considerations in quantum finance, engaging in ongoing research and discussions to adapt and refine our practices in line with evolving technology and societal values. By doing so, we can harness the tremendous potential of quantum finance to enhance financial decision-making and help build a more equitable and prosperous future for all.

Chapter 12: The Future of Quantum Wealth

Delving into the potential future developments and applications of quantum wealth, shaping the financial landscape.

As we enter into the era of quantum wealth, it is essential to consider the various advancements and transformations that lie ahead. Quantum technology, with its extraordinary computing power and mind-bending properties, is poised to revolutionize our approach to finance and redefine wealth creation. In this chapter, we will explore some of the potential future developments and applications of quantum wealth, offering a glimpse into the exciting possibilities that await us.

One area where quantum wealth promises immense potential is in the optimization of investment strategies. With its ability to perform complex calculations at unparalleled speeds, quantum computers can analyze vast amounts of data and uncover patterns that would otherwise remain hidden. This could lead to the development of sophisticated algorithms capable of predicting market trends with astonishing accuracy. Investors armed with quantum technology may gain unprecedented insights, enabling them to make more informed decisions and maximize their financial returns.

Furthermore, quantum wealth has the potential to reshape the way we secure our financial assets. Traditional security systems could become obsolete in the face of quantum computing's immense computational power. Quantum encryption, or qubit-based cryptography, could offer an unbreakable layer of protection, ensuring the confidentiality and integrity of financial transactions. The decentralized nature of blockchain technology may also benefit from quantum algorithms, reinforcing its robustness and enhancing trust in digital currencies.

In addition to investment optimization and enhanced security, the concept of quantum wealth may extend its influence to areas such as artificial intelligence and machine learning. Quantum technology could empower AI systems, enabling them to process information and learn at an exponential rate. This could lead to the development of advanced financial models capable of generating real-time predictions and adapting to dynamic market conditions, ultimately increasing profitability for individuals and businesses alike.

Moreover, the concept of quantum wealth may extend beyond traditional financial assets. As our understanding of quantum physics advances, the potential for the creation of novel quantum-based financial instruments arises. These instruments could leverage the principles of entanglement and superposition, allowing investors to explore untapped markets and embrace entirely new ways of generating wealth. Imagine the possibilities of quantum derivatives or quantum-based lending mechanisms, where financial transactions are influenced by quantum states, unlocking entirely new avenues for growth.

In conclusion, the future of quantum wealth holds unprecedented potential for transforming the financial landscape. The optimization of investment strategies, the fortification of security measures, and the integration of quantum technology with artificial intelligence are just a few examples of the groundbreaking changes we can anticipate. Furthermore, the emergence of quantum-based financial instruments opens doors to uncharted territories in wealth creation. Exciting times lie ahead, and in the second half of this chapter, we will delve deeper into these possibilities, exploring how quantum wealth intertwines with our everyday lives and unlocks new frontiers of financial potential. Are you ready for the quantum revolution?

In the second half of this chapter, we dive deeper into the exciting possibilities that quantum wealth offers, exploring its potential impact on various aspects of our everyday lives and uncovering new frontiers of financial potential.

One area ripe for transformation by quantum wealth is the field of risk assessment and management. Traditional risk models often rely on simplifications and assumptions that fail to capture the complexities of real-world scenarios. However, with the power of quantum computing, financial institutions can develop sophisticated models that consider a multitude of variables and interactions, allowing for a more accurate assessment of risks. By leveraging the computational capabilities of quantum computers, institutions can optimize portfolio allocations and minimize potential losses, ultimately leading to a more resilient and sustainable financial system.

Additionally, quantum wealth has the potential to revolutionize payment systems and transaction speeds. Traditional financial transactions, especially those involving cross-border transfers, can be time-consuming and costly due to the need for intermediaries and complex verification processes. Quantum technology has the potential to streamline these processes, enabling near-instantaneous and secure transactions through quantum networks. With quantum-based payment systems, individuals and businesses can enjoy faster and cost-efficient transactions, fostering greater economic growth and global connectivity.

Another area where quantum technology holds immense promise is in the field of financial inclusion. Quantum wealth has the potential to bridge the gap between the unbanked or underbanked populations and the global financial system. By leveraging quantum-based encryption and secure quantum networks, individuals in remote or underprivileged areas can securely access financial services, enabling them to save, invest, and participate in economic activities with confidence. This democratization of access to financial resources can empower individuals and communities, driving economic growth and reducing inequality.

Furthermore, the concept of quantum wealth extends beyond monetary transactions. With the integration of quantum technology, we may witness the emergence of decentralized and transparent systems for identity verification and authentication. Quantum-based biometrics, such as quantum DNA sequencing or quantum fingerprinting, can provide unprecedented levels of security and ensure privacy in an increasingly interconnected world. Trustworthy and tamper-proof digital identities could unlock new opportunities for individuals, facilitating access to services, healthcare, and education on a global scale.

Lastly, the potential of quantum wealth to drive sustainable finance and impact investing cannot be overlooked. With the ability to process vast amounts of data and simulate complex scenarios, quantum computers can facilitate the development of sophisticated models for assessing the environmental and social impacts of investments. This could lead to the emergence of quantum-based metrics and frameworks that enable investors to make more informed decisions aligned with their sustainability goals. Quantum wealth has the potential to catalyze the transition towards a more sustainable and equitable global economy.

In conclusion, the second half of this chapter has delved into the numerous ways in which quantum wealth can transform our financial landscape. From optimizing risk management and revolutionizing payment systems to fostering financial inclusion and driving sustainable finance, the possibilities are immense. As we harness the power of quantum technology, we must also ensure ethical and responsible deployment, addressing potential challenges such as quantum security threats and societal implications. The future is bright, and with the continued exploration and development of quantum wealth, we can unlock new avenues of financial potential, shaping a more prosperous and inclusive future. Welcome to the quantum revolution.

Dear Reader,

I want to extend my heartfelt thanks to you for taking the time to read this book. Your curiosity and willingness to explore the ideas and insights within these pages mean the world to me.

Writing a book is a journey of passion and dedication, and it's readers like you who make that journey truly meaningful. Whether you were seeking knowledge, inspiration, or simply a good story, your decision to pick up this book is a testament to your thirst for understanding and growth.

I hope that the words you've found within these pages have been enlightening, empowering, and, most importantly, enjoyable. Books have a unique ability to transport us to different worlds, challenge our perspectives, and enrich our lives, and it's my sincere hope that this book has done just that for you.

As an author, I am profoundly grateful for the opportunity to share my thoughts and ideas with you. Your support and engagement mean more than words can express. Please know that your time and attention are cherished, and your feedback, if you choose to share it, is invaluable.

Thank you once again for embarking on this literary journey with me. May the knowledge gained from these pages continue to inspire and guide you in your own journey through life.

With deepest gratitude,

Ben Davis

Thankyou

Thank you for your purchase! If you enjoyed this book, please consider dropping me a review. It take 5 seconds and helps a small business like mine.